Dorothy T. Samuel, a woman of many talents, is commentator for WBAL-TV in Baltimore, Maryland, and a free-lance writer with many books and articles to her credit. She earned her B.A. from Douglass College in New Brunswick, N.J., and her M.A. at The Johns Hopkins University in Baltimore, Md. For many years she has been concerned with the development of inner and personal peace and has worked with young people in and out of the church on attitudes of nonviolence. Even with her busy schedule, Ms. Samuel finds time for such groups as the Women's Rights Committee and the League of Women Voters and is a member of the English Curriculum Committee for the Baltimore Public Schools.

Safe Passage
on City Streets

Safe Passage
on City Streets

Dorothy T. Samuel

Nashville Abingdon Press New York

Safe Passage on City Streets

Copyright © 1975 by Dorothy T. Samuel

Library of Congress Cataloging in Publication Data

SAMUEL, DOROTHY T.
  Safe passage on city streets.
    1. Crime prevention. 2. Criminal psychology. 3. Interper-
sonal relations. I. Title.
HV7431.S24   232.9'7   74-19262

ISBN 0-687-36743-3

MANUFACTURED BY THE PARTHENON PRESS AT
NASHVILLE, TENNESSEE, UNITED STATES OF AMERICA

"THE FEAR OF CRIME is destroying some of the basic human freedoms which any open society is supposed to safeguard—freedom to walk the streets and to be secure in our homes, freedom of movement, freedom from fear itself."

—Herbert B. Newberg, CLASP

"We can greatly increase our chances of dominating any encounter with the frustrated and the alienated and the confused who have no weapon against society but violence and threat and brutality. . . ."

—*Safe Passage on City Streets*

Contents

Introduction

The largest prison in America has no bars, no locks, and no guards. The inmates are absolutely free to go anywhere they want at any time they choose. They may entertain anyone at all in their prison, and they are free to use force in denying entrance to those they do not welcome.

No accurate statistics exist to tell the exact number of persons so imprisoned. This is not only because the number is so large and increasing so rapidly. No statistics exist because these prisoners are all serving indeterminate sentences. They are all serving self-imposed sentences. These prisoners are serving sentences that only they can terminate.

Type histories will help identify those prisoners each of us knows personally.

There is the baseball fan who has imprisoned himself because he is afraid of the bus ride to night games.

The symphony lover who has imprisoned

himself because he is afraid to walk from the parking lot anymore.

The active church committeewoman who has imprisoned herself because she is afraid to park on the open street anymore.

The schoolgirl who has imprisoned herself because she is afraid to walk to the library in the evening anymore.

The lonely senior citizen who has imprisoned himself because he is afraid to walk to his friend's house after dark anymore.

The theatergoer who has imprisoned herself because she is afraid to wait for a taxi on the streets anymore.

There are the lovers who have imprisoned themselves because they are afraid to ramble in the park, and the bicyclist who is afraid to ride alone, the people who have given up night jobs, and the speakers who have cancelled evening engagements, the civic-minded who have stopped attending meetings, and the playful who have declined all party invitations.

These and millions of other formerly outgoing people have sentenced themselves to indefinite imprisonment within their homes and apartments behind locked doors and barred windows, where they press their noses against the glass of a television screen to watch distorted pictures of the life they once lived as free men and women.

And those who wish to be in prison, but dare not—the night nurse whose duty cannot be changed, the evening-school teacher, the all-night diner wait-

ress, and the letter carrier and insurance collector
—they walk in frightening isolation because those
others who might have been their companions on
the streets have chosen prison behind their own
locked doors. Every one who enters this prison existence increases the danger for those not yet imprisoned, increases the likelihood of another and yet
another resigning from free citizenry to take up the
life of the jail.

Nothing, of course, can make us wholly free from
danger, neither danger of attack nor danger of injury
during attack. Human life has never been free from
danger, nor will it ever be. No way of life, no system
of belief, no psychological techniques, and no defensive equipment or tactics can guarantee that one
shall walk unscathed from cradle to grave.

But we can get out of jail. The locks and bolts of
the soul can be unfastened, the bars of fear in the
mind unscrewed. Tunnels can be dug beneath the
walls of suspicion and distrust around the heart. We
can rechannel the very imagination which gives
human beings anticipatory fear experienced by no
other animal. We can use creative imagination to
program ourselves for freedom, for constructive in-
terpersonal relations, for daringly human responses
one to another, for biological and spiritual kinship.

Here are stories of those who have: great giants of
religious faith, spectacularly determined humanists,
unwavering servants to a chosen cause, and ordinary
people with no invisible supports of faith or dedication or even talent. They have met threat with some
inner confidence that breaks down the will of the

violent and at times even restores attackers to decency. Their experiences form a counterbalance to the oppressive horror of newspaper reports and crime statistics.

One of them may die tomorrow. Gandhi fell before the bullet of an assassin. But the experiences of these people, most of them quite ordinary individuals, do have some things in common. They are far less vulnerable to the universal dangers, and they are free from the prison of fear while they do walk this earth. And in their experiences, we glimpse the principles by which human beings gain control of their world and their own consciousnesses.

Trust Us

In 1972, two quite ordinary young women in Philadelphia walked out one night to pay their rent. They carried neither bag nor purse; having paid the rent, they drifted home penniless, rather obviously penniless. Yet, on the dark, empty city street, they were suddenly confronted by a tall youth who held a knife to the throat of the one nearer him.

"I want money. I have to have money."

It does happen on the streets today—the pain-crazed junkie desperate for a "fix." And, having made an approach, quiet retreat becomes for him the certainty of sudden chase by alerted police with screaming sirens and flashing lights and unholstered guns. The stickup is not a business where one can turn from a poor prospect and calmly seek a more promising customer.

As long as we have a society in which existence for some is so miserable that they would rather blank out than adjust, these confrontations will occur. No one can avoid all contact with the dropouts from cooperative living; even in self-chosen prisons, we are not invulnerable to invasion.

But we can prepare ourselves to face these situations. We can armor ourselves *inside*, prepare an impregnable identity which does not grovel before threat, nor lose all initiative in human encounter. We can carry our own world and our own values within us, project them around us. We can greatly increase our chances of dominating any encounter with the frustrated and the alienated and the confused who have no weapon against society but violence and threat and brutality.

We may not always succeed—there is no magic formula by which every human being can always prevail against any of the dangers of existence. Some people, however, have dominated danger situations, walked away unhurt against all predictable odds. Studying these people is far more healthful than allowing the literature of attack and murder and rape to incapacitate one's consciousness and habits. Looking for the common principles underlying their responses to danger can help us fantasize our own creative reactions. We can thus develop a bank of positive images for our reflexes to draw upon in sudden emergencies.

In this spirit, we observe two normal, unspectacular, unprepared young women in their early twenties, both small and rather soft, both constrained by the need to support the other. Were either to flee, they recognized at once, the other would fall to the knife. This very normal love determined their first choice: *I will not sacrifice my friend for myself.*

Love is a self-feeding explosion, just as fear is. Perhaps this first, almost instinctual, release of love set the course for their whole response pattern, even to the junkie threatening them.

"I don't want to do this," he began protesting. "I don't like to hurt people. But sometimes I have to!" The knife moved closer. "And if I have to, I will now. If I don't get money, someone is going to get hurt."

"But we don't have any money!"

"I have to have money!"

They began thinking of alternatives for him. None of them would do.

"If I don't get money, you'll get hurt."

"Look," said the smaller one, chin firm over the knife, "I'll stay here with you. Let Mary go back to my apartment and get you the money."

"No way! She'll call the cops."

"No, she won't! Really she won't. And I'll be here. She wouldn't call the cops while I was still here."

Still no one on the street. The three stood in an intimate little drama, knife blackened to avoid the light. A strange understanding began to grow in the young women. He really *didn't* like to do this. He really *was* miserable. He was also irrational. And more frightened, really, than they.

"Look, you come back with us. I have some money in my apartment. You come with us."

"No! Your husband will be there. Some man will be there." The jerky threat of the knife again.

"There's no one there. Honestly. The apartment is empty. Look, trust us. We'll get you the money."

15

"You'll call the fuzz."

"Trust us. Come on, we'll all go."

"It's a trick."

"It's no trick."

Was he weakening? His position was as futile as theirs—more futile. They simply had no money to give him there on the street. Bluster as he might, he could not make them produce what they did not have. And hurting them would not really help. He was in an impossible situation, and that terrible futility added to his crazed frustration.

"Look, trust us." She spoke to him directly, person to person—looked him in the eye, one human being to another. "I live just at the corner. Come along to the apartment."

He was wavering.

"There is no one there. Trust us. Come on."

Slowly, knife at the ready, he began to move along the dark street with them. The young woman kept talking quietly, normally.

At the outer door, he held back again, pulled her nearer to the knife.

"Just upstairs. There's no one there. Just trust us."

Inside the foyer. Up the stairs. Key in the lock. And the other young woman took over the position under the knife while the smaller one went into her apartment and rummaged for her purse. Ten dollars. A ten-dollar bill was the only money she had.

She ran back to the door, thrust it at him.

"Is that all you have?"

A sudden sinking feeling. After all this, after the appearance of trust, the seeming solution of their predicament, was he going to demand more? She had no more. And her apartment door stood open behind her.

"That's all. That's really all."

"But I only need five dollars. I don't have change."

From threat to apology. The role of crook had been lost when the young women refused the role of terrified victims.

"Take it. Take it. That's all right."

"But I only need five . . ." His hands were shaking, his voice trembling.

"That's all right. Take it. Take it."

He looked down at the bill, back into the young woman's eyes.

"Bye," she said. "Bye now."

And he slithered down the steps and out into the night. The young women collapsed on the couch, frightened now as they had not been under stress. Yet oddly elated, oddly concerned about the young man to whom they had come so close.

"He was so miserable!"

"Out of his mind!"

"So scared."

For of course he was scared. Scared of the tremors. Scared to pull a stickup. Scared of being caught. Scared, most of all, of the absolutely unknown. Scared of people who refused to meet him with responses he understood. When a man has geared himself to hate and threaten and even murder, what can he say in the face of a simple, human response? What can he do with two young women who say "Trust us"?

A reporter once quoted the British sergeant in charge of a platoon blocking the road against one of Gandhi's nonviolent but implacable acts of mass civil disobedience. The police and the satyagraha forces alike were knee-deep in flood water, the British troops on short-hour duty because of the difficulty and the danger of the rising waters. Gandhi's patient followers, on no such short hours, had been helping to right the overturned police boats, coming to the aid of the flooded British troops.

"If they fought back, if they used weapons, I'd know how to handle them," the distraught sergeant declared. "But this is something I don't understand."

Similarly, "trust us" was a response the junkie did not understand, a response for which he was not programmed.

Human Nature

Attack and confrontation did not begin in 1960. In the early days of the century, when thousands of immigrants crowded into an America whose language they did not know and whose customs baffled them, crime also ran wild on the streets of the new industrial cities.

One of the earliest to respond to the needs of these impoverished, often unemployed, workers was Jane Addams. In reverence for her social service, we often forget that she met personal attack, threat, and abuse. Hull House was converted for service work, but it was converted from a mansion and carefully maintained to provide an oasis of beauty for people forced to live in cramped, ugly tenements. To many a destitute and desperate immigrant, Hull House seemed the very essence of wealth and aristocracy.

One such man entered the house one dark night, making his way into Jane Addams' very bedroom to steal the wealth that he thought must be hidden in such a place. His presence woke Miss Addams, who might well have been terrified there in the slums of Chicago. Instead, her greeting was natural and instinctive.

"What do you want?"

"I want money."

"Well, what is the trouble?" she asked, just as she asked all needy callers.

"I need money. I'm out of work."

"I have no money. But if you will come around in the morning, I'll try to find a job for you."

The night was black in the room, the streets silent outside. She truly had no money, but she must have known the impression made by the beautiful furnishings and imposing structure of Hull House. However, she offered no explanations or protestations. And so natural and human was her response that the burglar did not doubt her word. He left.

Unthreatened, he left. And, unthreatened, he returned in the morning and identified himself. He was met not by police, but by the same calm woman of the night who did, indeed, find him employment. Person to person, fearlessness and integrity overcame the desperation, the frustration, the criminal intent of her visitor.

Jane Addams is, of course, one of the "greats" of our human heritage. Other people, too, are motivated so strongly by the desire to serve that their responses transform those who attack them. Calhoun Geiger, by a most amazing set of coincidences, was twice threatened by the same criminal, and turned double jeopardy into double opportunity.

Farming in Florida in 1947, he was confronted suddenly by an escapee from a convict gang. The man flourished a mattock and demanded money. A farmer in the fields has no money, and running from a desperate criminal is both risky and humiliating. Calhoun decided to talk, and the obvious strain and weariness on the convict's face readily drew from him real sympathy and concern for the misery of work-gang life.

In this atmosphere, the convict relaxed. Their talk became positive, conversational. In time the man declared he would return to jail, finish his sentence, and try to make something of his life. Calhoun went back to plowing.

Calhoun Geiger moved about in various service jobs. In 1952, he was directing a boys' club in Jacksonville. While driving home from work one night, he came upon a two-car collision where one driver was pounding the other, already unconscious, with a wrench. He jumped from his own car and clamped his arms around the attacker from behind. Despite the violent resistance and cursing of the man, Calhoun hung on. They fell to the pavement, but he did not let go; neither did he make any attempt to injure the man he was restraining. When at last the police arrived and took the man away, Calhoun had barely seen his face. Certainly he had not recognized him.

In 1955, Calhoun was working in the psychiatric ward of a hospital. One day the hospital director brought him a watch and told him the strange story of a man who had called and asked her to give the watch to Mr. Calhoun Geiger. He had identified himself as the escaped convict, and also as the infuriated driver on the road. He had not been able to stay straight after his release from prison, and indeed, it was the load of contraband whiskey in his car that had caused him to react so violently to the accident. But he had recognized Calhoun Geiger, and later been tremendously grateful that he had been prevented from adding murder to his crimes.

In 1968, he popped up again in Geiger's life. The newspaper in Greensboro, where Calhoun was then working, received and printed a letter which this man had sent in the hope that it would come to Calhoun's attention. He detailed his confrontations, the psychiatric treatment he had sought after his murderous rage on the street, the education he had then won, and his present job as a schoolteacher. All this he attributed to Calhoun Geiger, whose movements and locations he had carefully followed all through the years.

Not all of us will have the invincible good will of Calhoun Geiger. Not all of us are as dedicated to service as Jane Addams, nor as daring as Muriel Lester who took the arm of the leader of a mob beating up her meeting, asking and receiving his escort. Not all of us, like Helen Keller, can project reverent harmlessness even upon surly lions. But surely all of us can be as level-headed and compassionate as two young women on a Philadelphia street.

For the Logical

Just before Thanksgiving, 1972, the National Safety Council estimated that between 580 and 680 persons would die in holiday traffic accidents, and that another 30,000 would suffer disabling accidents. These figures were printed in newspapers across the country. Yet the nation hit the road as expected; old people, sick people, lone people, and people taking their small children.

In 1971, the murder rate for the United States averaged out to forty-five per day. There would likely be 180 murders over a four-day period, but more than 600 deaths by automobile. The number of murders, however, is drawn from the entire population, giving each man, woman and child statistically equal odds of $\frac{180}{200,000,000}$ over a four-day period —one in over one million. The automobile fatalities occur only to a much smaller number of people who are in automobiles. Instead of being 580–680 in two hundred million, the odds must be figured at

580–680 in the number of Americans on the road.

The same gross disparity in odds applies to injuries. There were about 1,000 assaults per day in 1971, 4,000 over any probable four-day period. Of these, only a small percentage resulted in injuries as serious as a broken limb. Yet Thanksgiving weekend produces 30,000 disabling injuries!

However, had any research council been able to predict that, in a given four-day period, deaths and disabling accidents from street crime would peak, the city streets of the nation would have been emptied for those four days. As during riots, ordinary citizens would have cowered in their homes, ventured out only when absolutely necessary—if possible with companions, and certainly without their small children.

There is something irrational about many people's fear of criminal attack. Certainly it is not irrational to fear danger, death, or mutilation. Prudent people respect real danger; they avoid it where possible, and prepare themselves to cope with it when it must be faced. But all living involves a certain amount of danger; even those who stay home in bed risk falling out, burning up, or developing bed sores.

The irrational factor is in fearing something inordinately, or in fearing small danger more than great danger. An astronaut who feared to ride a bicycle would seem ridiculous. A jockey who was afraid of riding escalators would seem obsessed. What then of people who will casually drive the freeways at Thanksgiving but fear to walk to the corner mailbox?

True, people are injured on bicycles, and some

24

legs have been broken stumbling on moving stairs. Some people have been assaulted going to the neighborhood mailbox. But almost everyone has either been in an automobile accident or known someone who has. Despite the rising crime rate, many of us have very little personal experience with street crime, and almost none with disabling results from street crime. Whole families have lived a lifetime in one city neighborhood without ever being subjected to personal attack.

Of those families where crime has struck, most have not really been the victims of random crime. Total crime statistics, as police and reporters well know but ordinary citizens do not, are a most inaccurate gauge of the dangers of walking to the mailbox. FBI statistics show that the percentage of crimes of violence committed by people known to the victims—relatives, friends, acquaintances, co-workers—keeps hovering at about 70 percent of all crimes of violence. Only 29 percent of such crimes involve complete strangers. More realistic to barricade oneself in the office and refuse to go home at night than to refuse to leave one's house.

The danger of being assaulted by a stranger simply because one happens to be on the street is thus only 29 percent as large as overall crime statistics would lead one to expect. The odds for death or crippling on the highways are subject to no such diminution.

It is true that some people are "accident prone," and seem to suffer far more than their proportion of accidents. The non-accident prone, therefore, have a lesser risk of serious accident. But this odds disparity is wholly due to mental, emotional, and physical qualities *of the victims.* Fearfulness, nervousness, despondency, anger all contribute to accident-prone driving. Psychologists write of subconscious death wishes and unconscious aggression acted out behind the steering wheel even when the driver is not consciously aware of these determinants.

The same preconditioning seems to predispose some people to victim status on the sidewalks. I talked recently with two women who live in the same rising crime area, live less than three blocks apart. One is a pleasant, kindly, reasonably active woman in her sixties; the other a healthy modern young married woman in her early twenties. Neither is strikingly unusual in any external way.

The older woman told me she no longer leaves her apartment after dark, never rides buses, and will not walk the two blocks to church on gray days. Yet she has had her purse snatched two or three times, and has felt threatened by young boys from whom she fled back into the apartment foyer. She feels driven to move from the neighborhood where she has lived since being widowed even though she will have to exchange a comfortable, well-equipped apartment house for something less attractive in the higher rent suburbs.

The younger woman, on the streets far more often and running to meetings and friends day and evening, was also talking about the city's burgeoning crime rate. But she concluded her generalities with the simple assurance, "There is no crime in this neighborhood."

Wherein lies the difference? It is true that the older woman's slower step and weaker reflexes might make her seem more vulnerable—thus more likely a victim. The young woman, however, is small and slight, and she is certainly far more likely to attract the sexual molester. Rape is one of the crimes which has increased in that neighborhood area according to police reports.

If the difference between the women is only age, then it is age's effect upon the attitudes dominating each, not age's effect on their limbs and muscles. In the same general neighborhood there lives another elderly lady, in her seventies, who continues to bus all over the city to keep up with her clubs and lectures and luncheons. Regardless of weather or hour, she will set out on excursions requiring two or three bus changes and walks of eight or ten blocks between discharge point and destination. She has never been bothered, and she turns indiscriminately to the nearest passerby for directions and aid. Age has not made her an invitation to muggers.

During the years of the White House Daily Vigil, a round-the-clock presence that drew people from all over the United States, a strange predictability was observed. Those participating were "crashing" in the poorest neighborhoods, walking to and from and through high crime areas. They were on the streets at all hours of the day and night. They were alike, too, in attitudes, for all had come because of overwhelming conviction that conflicts could be peacefully resolved.

Very few of them suffered any attack or holdup at

all. But, more noteworthy, those who did, suffered repeated incidents. And the longtime organizer who described all this had been struck by certain intangible but pervasive "atmospheres."

"One gets so he knows when they arrive," he mused, "who is going to be held up or knocked down." Nothing obvious, of course. He could not describe any signs or tangible characteristics. But somehow he was able to sense something in the "vibes" of those people who were victim-prone —something roaming criminals sense too.

These "vibes" distinguish the three women described. The elderly woman who is about to move out of her comfortable and convenient apartment is one of the nicest people I know. To know her is to love her. She is not reaping any "just reward" or being struck down by some cosmic retribution. She has allowed fear to dominate her imagination until the possibility of injury is more real to her than the pleasure of mobility.

The other elderly woman is dominated by the positive. When asked about the dangers inherent in her city-wide rambles, she snorts impatiently.

"The worst they can do is kill me! And I couldn't live anyway cooped up inside four small walls." Impatiently she puts crime out of her mind. Her mind is filled with the next speaker she looks forward to hearing, or the friends she expects to meet at a luncheon, or the sheer logistics of getting from northeast to southwest with the shortest wait between buses. "The coward dies a thousand deaths, the brave man only one."

The greatest injury done by today's street criminals has been to make cowards of us all—or many of us. Sometimes it almost seems, reading of some random, senseless, profitless exploit, that this is their intent—to seize psychological domination of a society over which they have no traditional tools of power; to manipulate and enslave by one thousand freakish assaults a day a people who are undeterred by thirty thousand disabling accidents in Thanksgiving traffic.

A World of One's Own

Although they make up a disproportionately large percentage of attackers, young people seem also to make up a disproportionately small percentage of victims of street crimes. While it may be claimed that young people generally will be thought to have less money, this is a specious argument for two reasons.

Addicts desperate for "fix" money take on the first comer. In deprived areas, welfare clients, cleaning women, elderly pensioners, and others who are obviously poor are attacked simply because they are available. Young people compare favorably with these prospects.

And young people are most available of all, for they comprise the only segment of the population that continues to stroll the streets. They go into high crime areas for programs and movies and parks, while older citizens sit home. College students stay late at libraries, and they take part-time night jobs. Many young people, particularly young women, deliberately volunteer for duty at various service agencies proliferating in high-crime areas: free clinics, drug abuse centers, drop-in centers, counseling centers. All of these activities require them to go and return at lonely night hours. Increasing numbers of young adults and couples are deliberately moving into apartments and rooms in the blight areas of large cities.

Gathering illustrations for this book, I was struck by the preponderance of youth among those who had faced danger and come away unscathed, whether the stories came from newspapers, books, or personal conversations. I was also struck by the number of young adults living in high-crime areas who assured me that they personally had never had reason to be fearful—no one had ever bothered them.

Talking with residents of a high drug section next to a university and overlapping the inner-city crime district has provided me with many examples. One older woman has three times had her purse snatched, although she comes into the section at night only once a month to attend a committee meeting. Some older people in apartment houses have been knocked down and robbed. Yet the dozens of students and the young workers who prefer to continue living in the active university area are scornful when asked about danger. They are on the same streets every day and every night, but not one has told me of an attack or confrontation. Some do not even lock their apartment doors; others buzz the opener for every ring of the doorbell.

These younger people are not better people; they are not as a group kinder or wiser or more religious or decenter than the older people to whom I talked. In some cases, they seem less so; experience and suffering have not yet smoothed the rough edges of their personalities. Certainly one's likelihood of being a crime victim is not related to any of these qualities in a simple "get what you deserve" sense.

But victimization does not seem to be mere random accident either. The correlation with age indicates that some quality weakens as we grow older, or that some new attitude tends to develop, if we are not aware and controlling our maturation.

The young are not blind to the facts of street life. They are probably more aware, as their service in volunteer ghetto programs and drug clinics and run-away houses indicates. They differ in response to facts rather than in knowledge of facts. They are quick to sympathize with underdogs; the deprived, the addicted, the unhappy, the sick. They believe in people and the possibility of their rehabilitation. Because they identify with the lost and the suffering and the rebellious, they relate to them as human beings wherever they meet them. They do not have two categories: people you can treat as people, and people who are only animals. They are not yet cynical, neither are they judgmental.

And the young still have great confidence in their own invulnerability. They do not expect anything really bad ever to happen to them. They also take

32

very literally the American promise of personal freedom of action, and liberty to pursue happiness as
one chooses. They are wrapped in their own inviolable right to go where they want when they want and
how they want.

These qualities are not majestic or saintly. They
often lead to brash behavior, dangerous carelessness,
and downright obnoxious self-absorption. They also
lead many young people to spontaneous actions and
reactions disruptive of criminals' game plans, and to
ways of carrying themselves which deflect criminal
intent.

There can be no persuasive anecdotes of the latter.
If I walk down the street past a lurking mugger and
he does not attack me, I have no story to tell. I did not
know he was a mugger; I did not know he decided to
wait for another victim. Although prevention is
more desirable than cure, the principles of prevention can only be inferred from the case histories of
cure. We cannot make a laboratory of the street and
send one hundred people past a hidden attacker,
then analyze the personalities of those not attacked.

Despite the smaller number of young people attacked, however, we do find many stories of young
people turning off an attacker's plans. They simply
do not play his game. They see him as a person like
themselves, as the young women in Philadelphia
saw the junkie.

Or they respond out of their own sense of the
rightness of things as did one young bank trainee.
When the classic holdup man pushed the classic
holdup note into her teller's cage, she did not re-

spond to the gun cradled under a sheltering arm. He could not invade the righteousness of her own world, a world in which she lived with the absorption of the very young.

"You can't do that," she burst out, "it's against the law."

The naiveté is breathtaking. But it took the crook's breath too, and he ran from the bank, absolutely defeated by her inviolable innocence. What power could he bring against a girl who simply did not understand the world of theft and threat? He could hardly stand there and argue with her. He did not really want to shoot her in the middle of a bank with counter glass between him and the money anyway.

Of course, one cannot plan such moves ahead. No person who had thought out exactly what she would say to a bank robber could possibly burst forth with a statement like that. But one can plan and program her or his consciousness; one can choose the mental and emotional world in which he will live. When emergencies erupt, one answers out of that mental and emotional world.

In another city, a young woman showed a very similar confidence in her own sense of the rightness of things. She had no bank room around her, no co-workers or patrons to dash to her aid. But she inhabited much the same inner world as the bank teller.

Coming home alone on a tree-shaded street, she was stopped by a youth brandishing a knife carefully blackened against stray beams of light. This was no inexperienced holdup man. Yet when he grabbed her and demanded her purse, she was affronted in her sense of the rightness of things.

"You can't bother me! This is my neighborhood!"

It sounds like a response out of "Laugh In" rather than reality. The young woman herself was aghast later when she told the story. But it worked. She was living in a world the attacker could not enter, and with nothing in the outer world to stop him from physical force, he turned and fled.

Acting from principle is a fine philosophy for great minds to examine. But action from any core of inner self, any bastion of selfhood, is a protection with which few mixed-up, petty crooks can cope. The confused collapse before the integrated, and the integration does not have to be based on greatness.

Sometimes it is based on nothing but pride, or even a kind of arrogance. Both represent a value on the self, an absolute rejection of thing-dom.

Another young woman, barely five feet of almost childish-looking frailty, was pushed against a wall in a lonely subway station by a boy obviously seeking some proof that he was a self. He was no more than ten or twelve, but tall as she and broader. Also he was armed. When he held a small pocketknife to her throat, he was appropriating the strength and power of a dozen TV images.

She stood still, glaring at him, affronted by his touching her. "You're afraid of me, aren't you?" he gloated.

Perhaps she should have been. Even the police would have told her she should have been. She was in an area overrun with young toughs, terrorized by senseless violence and brutality. But she was infuriated rather than terror-stricken, and she snapped back at him in his own jargon.

"The hell I am!"

"You'd better be afraid of me!" He waggled the knife before her eyes.

She spat a vulgar word at him.

The pitiful masque collapsed; the game ended. She was supposed to cringe, to twist and turn in futile escape, to cry or beg like some whining dog. There was no fun in this, no sense of power and mastery, no entry into a fantasy of personal superiority and importance.

With a grunt, the boy turned away and moved off down the platform.

This inner world is not, of course, limited to youth. It should, indeed, be stronger in older people who have had time to develop their own philosophy, their own habit patterns, their own outlook, their own inner resources. It should also be more self-conscious, more reliable, because it has been carefully chosen and painstakingly developed. When older people have fed their minds on thoughts that uplift, and trained their emotions on feelings that ennoble, they become invincible.

A man of peaceful concerns, a leader in activities to improve the ecology of our environment, lives by choice in a New York inner-city apartment. One night, returning late from a meeting, he opened the foyer door and moved toward the inner door to find that three large men had slipped in around him. One of them held a knife. They demanded money.

As he told me about it later, he said that he felt a strange sense of spiritual power and no fear at all. He looked the speaker directly in the eyes, and spoke to him frankly and firmly.

"I work for peace, and I don't *have* any money. And you will have to go." He then reopened the door through which they had all entered, and ushered them out.

Here is what age and maturity should mean. Not out of the arrogance of youth but out of the confidence of a life spent in service for spiritual goals, from an inner integration around his own principles, this man looked out at other men with understanding and even sympathy. His confidence sprang from spiritual power, not muscular superiority. And so he spoke fearlessly, man-to-man, without threat and without bombast. He spoke honestly, and honesty served him because he truly was living a sacrificial life in which he accumulated no money.

Maturity is the ennobling of youth's idealistic impulses through experience and thought and discipline, so that the hedonistic center of being is transformed into reasoned wisdom. Maturity should make us more understanding of human weaknesses, not just more aware of them; more skillful in reaching the good in others, not just more ready to deny it; more powerful in transforming evil, not just in punishing it. Maturity should turn brashness into quiet courage, and self-centeredness into personal integrity.

Old or young, principled or self-centered, there is a kind of baring of oneself in all these responses.

37

Youth bares itself because it has accumulated little of which to be ashamed; it can assume the attacker has little also—the present confrontation being an extremity which the other will shortly regret. Dedicated, mature people bare themselves, again human-to-human, because they have learned to live with their own weaknesses, and they have no intention of being infected by the weaknesses of any attacker.

That Old-Time Religion

An elderly woman, devout and pious, walked home one evening from a prayer group. They had focused that night on the reassurance of Psalm 91, that paean of security and faith. They had read it, prayed it, appropriated it. And they had parted singing the old hymn, "Under His Wings I Am Safely Abiding."

As she trotted along the dark street, a fantasy of herself lovingly clasped under a great wing of soft, protective feathers grew. She was barely aware of passing streetlights and darkened doors, for she was snuggling under that wing, feeling the power of that wing, absorbing the warmth of that wing.

Out from the darkness along her way stepped the classic holdup man with the classic holdup line, gun just visible in the hand close to his waist. The woman wrenched herself back from her avian experience, and some of the feathers were wrenched with her into the world of the mugger.

"You can't hurt me!" she burst out. "I am covered with his feathers!"

The cynical-minded may well say that the attacker fled fearing a madwoman. The devout may proclaim the reality of divine protection. The fact is the same: a fearless consciousness disrupted the whole mind-set, the entire game plan, of the criminal.

This is the mark of fearlessness, whether it springs from utter reliance on God, from complete self-confidence, or from instinctive empathy with the desperate. Fearlessness acts, it does not simply react according to conventional stereotypes. Fearlessness is always individual, unique, and unpredictable. Fearlessness confronts any situation with authentic personhood.

Much might be made of the different quality of life revealed by "I am covered with his feathers" and "You can't do that, it's against the law." Morally there is a vast gap between offering help to an attacker and spitting out, "The hell I am." But the responses are alike in fearlessness, and fearlessness breaks down any scenario. The program cannot play itself out. Attacker confronts not victim, not a mere thing; attacker confronts a living, feeling, autonomous human being. Attacker must himself become a living, feeling human being—or flee. To victims without Jane Addams' dedication to serving the delinquent, either is quite satisfactory.

Job proclaimed, "That which I fear has come upon me." Jesus said, "According to your faith it is done to you." Coué changed lives at the beginning of the century with a self-hypnotic technique based upon the principle that we actualize that upon which we fix our consciousness. Psychosomatic doctors tell us that people who live in dread of cancer are more likely to get cancer, fear of heart trouble can bring on cardiac attack. Insurance statistics prove that well over half the accidents happen to the same small group of people—over and over again.

We attract that which we fear; we attract what is in our consciousness; we attract the roles we dream about. We attract violence when we condition our minds violently, and we attract danger when we fill our minds with fear. The victim of three purse-snatchings described in an earlier chapter is no isolated freak of fate. She alone of the many members attending evening committee meetings was attacked three times; the others not at all. She is a beautiful person—warm, generous, good. It is no defect in her character that causes assault. But she walks in fear, intimidated by the news reports and magazine articles dramatizing the brutality of faceless "others" against whom she feels her gentleness would have no chance.

Potential criminals sense this mind-set as any dog knows the person who fears him. Dogs smell that fear. Even the calmest people-dog will bark ferociously when presented with a willing victim.

At one time we lived at the end of a long lane of faculty houses on which several dogs frolicked freely. Students, faculty, and outside visitors walked up and down that lane calling at various homes, and no one feared the dogs. No one ever had cause to fear the dogs.

Then a young city man with an obsessive fear of dogs arrived on campus. Sure enough, he was threatened every time he came to visit us.

People with an obsessive fear of other people bring out the fearsome in other people. When such frightened people happen, in the course of normal events, to pass by a real criminal, they will be attacked—and more viciously attacked than other victims. They seldom come out from an encounter unscathed because they fit so excellently the role of victim and thus lock the attacker into his own fantasy scenario of power and machismo.

It is this consciousness that religious faith transforms. There is no room for the imagination of oneself at the mercy of brutality when the mind is filled with consciousness of Godly power. Under his wings, protected as a chick by its mother, or empowered by divine commandment to accomplish some mission God himself wants to preserve, there is simply no recognition of personal impotence. Whether it be Jane Addams helping the burglar from her bed or the Indian mystic Sundar Singh stroking a man-eating leopard while he prays; whether it be Muriel Lester taking escort from the leader of a violent mob destroying her meeting or Helen Keller entering the lion's cage to "see" him with her hands, the consciousness of spiritual unity with all life creates its own aura. Criminals of both the human and animal world respond to this subtle fragrance as surely as they recognize the smell of fear.

Body Language

Two American college girls, cavorting through Mexico with that special freedom-high felt only in strange and glamorous places, demonstrated the accuracy with which signals are received on the street, received immediately by the very persons looking for trouble or adventure or crime.

They had taken a carefree ramble, heady with the exotic sights and sounds and smells of an alien city and its provocatively bizarre customs. They walked for hours along the crowded streets, rubbernecked at hovels and cathedrals, fingered endless displays of serapes and ponchos, tapestries and pottery. They ran, they giggled, they jostled; they laughed too loudly and whispered too obviously.

Reaching for ultimates, one exuberantly suggested, "Let's pretend we're prostitutes." She stepped into a doorway, thrust out a hip and bent one leg in a movie-learned flaunt. Before her companion could join the game, two men had stepped from the hundreds on the street and approached her with obvious intent.

We must remember that, unrestrained as their conduct had been during the long walk preceding this make-believe, they had moved among the crowds in safety and privacy. No one had accosted them; no one had approached them; no one had molested them. In less time than it takes to write the description, the scene changed. By a simple alteration of the way she carried herself, the young coed transmitted a message in the body language of the streets. Because she was in a crowd, interpreters were immediately beside her.

Actors live by body language. No voice says to the audience, "This woman is weary," or "This man is suppressing anger," or "This child is nervous." A movement, a gesture, a curve of the body—the vitality of the step or the height of the chin—these tell the audience that the character portrayed is dominated by one emotion or another, by one life-view or another.

Teachers, too, learn the effectiveness of body language if they are to make successful guides in a classroom. The sharpness of a look, the stiffness of a pointing finger, the tightening of body muscles, the moue of exasperation, all convey disapproval more forcefully than any amount of screaming or scolding or threatening. The lawyer in the courtroom feigning the little gestures of confidence, the bad boy grinning innocently, the pickpocket apologizing casually as he brushes by, and the doctor smiling calmly as he hears the fatal symptom—all know the importance of body language in communicating attitudes which will, in turn, determine the attitudes and actions of those watching.

What does our own, usually unconscious, body language convey? When we huddle into ourselves, slip from streetlight to streetlight, look back over our shoulders, and scuttle away at each approaching footstep, what is our body language broadcasting? Does it not proclaim that here is a timid, frightened creature who will put up little resistance—physical or psychological—and so will be easy to knock off for purse or wallet or to intimidate for rape or assault?

Fortunately, we walk most often on streets populated by other decent people, and this message goes unnoted or at least without response. But there are receiving stations. The teen-ager looking for an easy thrill, the junkie building up for a snatch, the petty thief alert for opportunities, all pass us occasionally. When they do, the message from our pose rings loud and clear: here is a perfect victim. If the other external conditions are right, we become another statistic; and we go our way more frightened than ever, transmitting even stronger signals the next day and the next and the next.

It is better to look brave when one is not than to out-picture invitingly the ideal victim. It is best of all really to be confident, to be so absorbed in healthy thoughts and activities that the body language naturally gives a true picture of inviolability. The sham will fall in that odd instance when attack does occur, when danger draws reaction from the true

45

inner self. But attack does not really confront us very often, and every day of exercising the body language of confidence contributes to the development of the inner reality. The practices of a lifetime mark the body and the muscles.

A retired schoolteacher visited New York City with great trepidation. She had allowed herself to picture New York as one great playground of criminals, and herself as an aged and weak woman. She had accepted the scoldings and the warnings of those who told her she was a fool even to venture into Fun City.

What she expected was delivered. On the last evening of her visit, she was indeed stopped on the sidewalk by a young hood who shielded a gun and demanded her money on threat of death.

The body language of a lifetime took over in crisis, trampling the mentality of her more recent absorptions. The old schoolteacher response drew her tall, and her eyes flashed with authority as she commanded, "Stop that at once! You put that gun away!"

And it was in the body language of chastized schoolboy that the delinquent dropped his gun-wielding hand, shrank into himself, and ran off down the street.

We become what we feed upon; the stance of command is developed by assuming leadership, and the acceptance of defeat by the habit of drawing back. Heroes are made by dreaming of heroics, and victims are made by imagining a thousand scenes of victimization. Opportunities come to those who look able to handle them, and rejections rain upon those who appear already beaten. The outside world reacts to the self we ourselves describe, but it reads that description in our less conscious and less censored body language rather than in our carefully guarded words.

Trust *Them*

When I go to Friends Meeting, I hear regularly that "there is that of God in every man." When I tune in a radio evangelist, I am assured that "Christ died for the least of these." When I read an ecumenical publication, I am reminded that we are all one, alike children of a single Father. The Jesus "freaks" urge us to love everyone, and the street missions instruct us to serve the stranger.

When I turn to the universities, I find students believing that the oppressed are more worthy—in some fundamental way, more *real*—than the people of privilege. Sociologists match the ascending curve of national corruption to the descending curve of people-power. Political scientists praise the instinctive wisdom of the "man in the street." Economists explain that criminality is forced upon basically decent people by gross inequities in distribution of national resources. Educators insist that no group is incapable of responding to learning and culture; we are all alike in inherited capacity.

Literature has long depicted the kindly prostitutes and the sentimental burglars, the generous cardsharpers and dog-loving gangsters. Musical interpreters offer songs of toil and the rhythms of the streets as reflections of the soundest, the truest, and the most deeply human spirit of the race.

Why, then, do we fear each other? Why do we cringe from the approaching stranger and fear the badly dressed, the poor, the idle, the different, or the foreign-looking? To the religious, these should be people of special preciousness; to the erudite, these should be living examples of the noble "wretched of the earth"; to the artistic, these should be simple saints relatively uncorrupted by the hypocrisy of status and society.

Why do we not trust that of God in the drifter? Why do we not rely on the fundamental decency of the poor? Why do we not seek the wisdom of the man on the street? Why do we not expect kindness from the petty criminal, and human warmth from society's dispossessed? Why are we not eager to investigate the different or the foreign? Why are we always surprised when we find exactly those good qualities in which we profess to believe?

A middle-aged, white, suburbanite woman recently shared an experience. A religious woman, like most of her listeners, she believed in that of God in everyone. Also like most of her listeners, she drove regularly through Harlem only in daylight, with her doors locked and windows tightly closed.

She always checked the gas gauge first, and she never stopped. In one compartment of her mind, she believed God was in each of these people; but in another compartment, she did not expect to meet him there.

On this occasion, she was returning from Columbia at about six o'clock in the evening, tightly insulated from the Harlemites as usual. On Lenox Avenue her car suddenly stalled and would not start again. Finally, she released the hood latch and reluctantly stepped out from her wheeled prison.

As she looked at the hundreds of black faces about her in the rush-hour traffic, her mind was overwhelmed with stories of muggings, assaults, rapes, and vicious, senseless beatings. She fumbled wildly, ignorantly, under the hood.

A middle-aged man detached himself from the black mass and asked if he could help. Then a young man came up, smart and strong and very confident—like a hundred movie toughs.

More afraid of saying no to these strangers than hopeful of help, she let them look under the hood. The younger man quickly told her that the water hose had broken, and that he could easily replace it if he had another.

Still terrified, she gave him the few dollars she had in her purse, went into a pay phone to call her husband, and returned to wait. It grew darker; she huddled in her disabled car; her husband did not arrive; she now had no money at all for garage service.

An hour passed, and she knew she had been taken.

People went by on the sidewalks, but she was locked away from them, afraid to appeal to any of them. Night was coming on when they could easily attack the car.

Suddenly the young man appeared walking down the street; from his hand dangled a hose.

"I'm sorry I took so long," he told her as she rolled down the window nervously. "I had to walk to three different places to find the right hose."

He set about making the replacement, started the car, and smiled at her happily. At that moment, her husband finally drove up and immediately offered to pay the young man—which he refused in neighborly fashion.

Why should the story be so surprising? Nothing occurred which our religion, our sociology, and our art have not memorialized for centuries. Nothing happened which was not in tune with the woman's own professions about human nature. Nothing happened, in fact, which does not happen thousands of times every day across the nation.

But we have let ourselves be hypnotized by the headlines describing aberrant behavior, vicious behavior, unhuman behavior. It is as if we were so paralyzed by the existence of salmonella bacteria that we refused to eat any food at all, or so terrified of the lurking bee that we never put our nose to the fragrance of a flower.

Most people *are* good. Most people really like to be of help. Most people want friendliness more than hostility. Most people like to make the world around them a little happier. All this human beauty we miss when we hide away from our fellows and contact them only with terror or threat.

And we live our lives in a schizophrenic division between what we believe and what we say we believe. We build blockages in our minds and obsessions in our emotions. Where we should be integrated personalities of seamless fabric, we are cue-geared disunities speaking and acting in erratic jerks according to the primacies of each moment.

A double-minded man, unstable in all his ways, will not receive anything from the Lord, James wrote many centuries ago in his epistle. Nor anything from other men, he might have added, nor from life itself. How many of us have lived in our little walled compartments, never blasted out by the accident of a broken hose to find the rich, full, human garden surrounding us? How many friends have we never met, how many speakers never heard, how many inspirations never gained, how many experiences never tasted because we kept our religious precepts or our intellectual knowledge or our artistic intuitions for oral expression, and lived by the murky terrors of newspaper faith?

A friend who lives by choice in a Brooklyn neighborhood so bad that he receives no mail in the constantly broken boxes of his apartment house, speaks of what he calls "trust vibrations." In any situation, he believes, it is possible to set up these trust vibrations and see humanity triumph over criminality.

To illustrate, he described an experience when he and a friend had a flat tire on a street reputed to be the most dangerous in the section. It was late at night, and the street was heavily populated with junkies and toughs.

A small crowd began to gather immediately. Yet he got out of his car in the consciousness of trust vibrations. One man immediately hurried off and returned with a jack; another ran into a building and came back with a large flashlight. Other men grabbed hold and jacked up the car; more hands changed the tires.

My friend was not surprised. Though he does not recommend recklessness, he firmly believes he can inject these trust vibrations into any situation which arises spontaneously, and that enough people walking in this consciousness would change the climate in our cities. He has put into practice the convictions which he speaks, and his life is a free one, consistent and of one piece—as all *peace* is of one piece.

What We Are

"Men do not attract what they want, but what they are," wrote Alice Steadman in a little book of psychosomatic and spiritual inquiry. The epigram has universal implication.

Men who purchase weapons for self-defense in the event of burglary, robbery, or assault, most certainly do not want these events to occur. Even more surely, they do not want to be injured themselves or have their families injured should criminals invade their privacy.

In one city, a candy store owner kept a gun beneath the counter of his store. He was not a vicious man, nor a violent man. Store owners up and down the street on which he did business were being subjected to frequent hits by young toughs; he had become a self-defensive personality. When the holdup came, however, there was no dramatic TV victory of virtue over crime. While one of the two holdup men held a hand gun on a customer in the store, the other vaulted the counter. The storekeeper pulled his gun. He never fired it; the armed gunman shot twice before the proprietor could pull his own trigger, and the storekeeper took two bullets in his head. His son, still playing out the game of self-defense, grabbed up the gun and fired repeatedly at the holdup man. It was not the righteous bullets that found their target, however, but return fire which felled the storekeeper's son.

For an ordinary citizen, firing at an armed intruder is practically suicide. Even those superhuman TV heroes, the Cannons and the Mannixes and the Kojacks, drop their weapons in gun-to-gun confrontation unless they can dive behind a protecting wall. Experts explain how difficult it is really to incapacitate a man by a single shot under the conditions of tension and quick movement which characterize criminal attack. The return bullet is often on its way before the criminal falls or dies. Even after receiving an instantly fatal wound, the body contracts with the involuntary muscle spasms which, police warn, can trigger a gun clutched in the hand.

The fascination with gun defense leads to completely meaningless injury and death. Quite typical are two youths who wanted neither injury nor violence. While visiting together, one displayed and demonstrated his gun collection. A .38 caliber revolver had accidentally been left loaded. The admiring friend pointed it at the owner's eye, and it went off dead on target. Of the deaths among gun owners between 1958 and 1972, 70 percent follow this pattern; they shot themselves or friends to death while "playing with" a weapon.

The argument from self-defense illustrates the terrible escalation of violence. Because crime increases, gun ownership increases. Because gun ownership increases, criminals go armed. As a result of this kind of vicious spiral, deaths by gun tripled between 1958 and 1972.

Detroit, in recent years dubbed the murder capital of the U.S. by *Newsweek* (January 1, 1973), illustrates this infinite progression of cause and effect. The riots of 1967 produced a wave of hysterical fear. Citizens rushed to the gunsmiths and brought into their homes and lives an unprecedented arsenal of handguns for self-defense. Police estimate that at least half a million handguns are now circulating, more than double the number held before 1967. Also since 1967, coincident with the rise of gun ownership, Detroit's homicide rate has doubled (homicide, not just criminal murder). At least 60 percent of these homicides involved handguns. And the spiral continues. Because the homicides increase, terrified citizens are buying more defensive weapons.

Some of these homicides result from attempts at self-defense and others from playing with weapons. A larger number, that 70 percent of homicides occurring among relatives and friends, are completely crimes of the moment. Two people who normally care for each other become involved in a really heated argument. Each hurls cruel words; each screams horrible accusations. Finally one remembers the gun carefully placed for defense against burglar or thief, and he grabs it up as man's ultimate declaration of supremacy. A shot, two shots, and someone lies bleeding or dead. Often the person who fired the shot is waiting in tears and remorse when the inevitable authorities arrive. Police feel helpless before this sort of crime—unpremeditated, emotional crime for no gain.

"If the cat didn't have a gun available when he got into an argument, he'd probably just (punch) the other person," said a tough sergeant. "The other guy might end up with a busted lip, but he'd still be alive." And, as he did not say, a man might be fined for assault, but he would not be put away for a life sentence.

The very presence of a gun or other weapon, however, indicates the sort of people we have become. We have allowed the violence of criminals to turn us into people of violence too. We feed on violence, their and our own fantasies of violent defense. And "men do not attract what they want, but what they are."

It takes courage to root our personal safety in the strength of our own character and life-style alone, but it also takes courage to pull a gun in the presence of an attacker. There is danger in reliance on our own ability to de-escalate violence, but there is danger in meeting violence with violence too. The transforming responses of great characters and the simple reactions of very ordinary persons, as well as the practical experiences of police officers, indicate that the lesser risk accompanies the more humane course. The wisdom of great spiritual leaders does not rest on its idealistic elevation, but upon its profound understanding and revelation of how the world actually works.

Police Realities

Police safety lectures are now emphasizing the dangers of self-defense. Unless a victim is prepared to go all the way—to gouge out an eye or break a bone, even to kill—he should offer no physical resistance, they say, no threat. Anything less, mere blows to the throat or scratches at the cheek or stamping on an instep, insure retaliation. The criminal is tough; he can absorb such minor pain. His own fear and his fury will respond with counter-violence that has no hesitation about maiming or killing—may even welcome that ultimate release.

As I write, the morning paper carries the report of a youth sentenced for stabbing a sixty-two-year-old woman to death. He was one of four young men who accosted her on a city street. They were unarmed.

> . . . When the woman attempt-
> ed to fend off her attackers
> with a knife she carried for

protection, she was disarmed
and stabbed seven times.

To add the final ironic note, society accused the youths only of second-degree murder because they had not come armed, and they pled "self-defense."

There was nothing prudent about this woman's providing a weapon for possible attackers. There was nothing wisely prudent about arousing their own fears, their self-defensive instincts.

Konrad Lorenz, who has made himself something of an international authority on aggression, describes also a basic human reaction mechanism that causes our species to draw back from ultimate cruelty. We have, he says in his article "Why Men Kill Other Men," an instinctive inhibition against killing and maiming other people or even human-like animals. But he is quite clear about the limits of this mechanism. "There is, however, one circumstance which, if it arises, extinguishes all our instinctive inhibitions against killing. Any trace of pity disappears instantly if we are in serious fear of the attacking animal—or human."

We see this in ourselves. It is our very fear of the criminal that induces the most peaceful among us to consider windpipe chops and groin kicks. It is fear that causes elderly woman to carry and then flourish knives. The criminal is the *least* peaceful of us! When he faces threat, when he has cause to fear one of us, his already weak inhibition against hurting others breaks down entirely. He hits or stabs or shoots as viciously and violently as he can, often madly continuing to punch or stab even after his victim is unconscious.

The director of a prerelease center for violent juvenile offenders illustrated how the best-trained rehabilitative personnel now act upon this principle. In the two years this school has served young criminals all of whom are hyperactive violents, there has been no incident of physical injury on the premises. He did tell, however, of the one body blow that marred their record.

A new teacher had been struck and knocked down. "But he had disobeyed our cardinal rule," the director smiled. "He just forgot."

The cardinal rule is that staff are never to stand between an offender and the door; no teacher is to position himself where he *seems* to cut off escape. In the minds of these violence-prone youths, even a casual pause before the exit may represent threat and entrapment. When that happens, the violent response is triggered though there has been no real threat offered.

Similarly, those most expert in defensive tactics and weaponry find themselves personally safer when they do not rely on those skills. The police of Louisville have been devising creative, human techniques to reduce the level of violence in situations where once they might have burst in with drawn weapons. Now, when called to homes where family members are beating or shooting at each other, the police deliberately enter casually, throw the scenario out of focus. They are trained and practiced in the

61

body movements, the conversation, the little human acts that remove threat and call for normal, friendly responses.

The FBI Uniform Crime Statistics show that one in four homicides occurs in just such family situations. Police departments report that a large percentage of injuries to officers occur when they must intervene in such family fights. Therefore, the Louisville department has developed a Crisis Intervention technique that depends for its success upon reducing the level of violence and threat, upon strengthening the innate inhibition against hurting others. They deal with battling family members as individuals, respectfully and sympathetically. In the opening experiment with this new approach, police responded to twelve hundred crisis calls without a single officer being attacked. Departments from Virginia to Texas are now studying and imitating the method, and the federal Law Enforcement Assistance Administration is subsidizing at least six communities in setting up similar Crisis Intervention training systems.

Not just the absence of threat, but positive bits of human interaction call upon a different role response in the combatants. In one situation, officers found an apartment almost wrecked, a knife lying on the coffee table, the wife bruised, the husband turning with curses to the intruding policemen. One officer quietly removed the knife, while another swept off his hat and asked pleasantly, "Mind if I smoke? Some people don't like the smell of cigars."

So simple an act of normal courtesy, most abnormal in such strained circumstances, often shifts the whole emotional scene. The level of interaction is jolted to a new dimension, habitual responses of politeness surface. One such break in the tension is all the officers need to begin constructive problem solving, separating the combatants in different rooms and really listening to each before offering any services or counsel.

One break in the tension, sudden destruction of the scenario of violence, may also be all an attacked individual needs to activate some more normal response pattern in his attacker.

An amusing incident of this sort occurred when a bone-tired waitress, alone just before closing a small cafe, was suddenly confronted by an armed intruder. He ordered her to give him the money from the register, but she just sat on where she was resting her feet.

"I'm sick," she complained. "I couldn't move if I had to."

There was nothing to prevent the gunman from opening the register himself; she was no threat; she wasn't even interested. But he left. Her simple, human, ordinary response threw off all his emotional preparation, perhaps appealed to his own experiences of fatigue.

This woman, unlike the police in Louisville, was not making a calculated psychological response. She was simply immersed in her own trouble, and she responded to an attacker in the same way she would have responded to a friend or a customer who made a demand on her at that moment. In so doing, the level of violence was reduced, the scenario rewritten.

Neither careful police planning nor instinctive human response will always work so simply. Registers will be robbed or purses taken; civilians or officers will sometimes be abused. The young women in Philadelphia lost ten dollars. But when police officers who know precisely how to use weapons decide it is safer to be nonthreatening, ordinary people might well reconsider the "practicality" of self-defense.

We do not attract what we want, but what we are. If we are programmed to help, like the Louisville Crisis Intervention officers or Jane Addams, in a different dimension, we attract the response given helpers. If we are firmly settled in a self of our own determining, like the ecology worker or even the young bank teller, that self will set the tone of the encounter.

Your Money or Your Life

Friends returned from a summer camping trip to find their house had been broken into and thoroughly ransacked. The first question we all asked was, "Did they take *everything?*" The couple exchanged peculiar glances.

"No," answered the husband. "No. They didn't take *anything.*"

"It gives you an odd feeling," the wife added dryly, "to realize there isn't anything in your house even thieves will bother with."

And they exchanged glances again; wry, a little embarrassed, but basically very satisfied.

These are not poverty-stricken people. The husband holds a responsible position in a nonprofit organization. He could earn much more for the same duties in private enterprise, but he is paid an adequate salary for simple living. The wife, educated and capable of earning money, is not at the moment employed outside the home because she prefers to remain with their young children. They do not live in a slum, nor are they lacking any of the really basic amenities of modern life. They have central heating, plumbing, refrigeration—even a TV, but an old and unattractive set passed down from relatives.

Their life-style says a great deal about the evidences which measure what people really believe, what values they really hold dear, what priorities govern their thinking and acting, and the indefinable aura by which they are accompanied. Other people, similarly choosing work they believe important in preference to high salaries, also live in simple housing on unimpressive streets where no clever burglar would waste his time. Only this couple, probably hit by some inexperienced gang, have been shown so very clearly that their material life-style actually repels crime.

Poverty alone, of course, is not a guarantee against robbery. Really desperate junkies under urgent fix stimulation will knock over even welfare recipients, knowing that such poor persons are actually more likely to be carrying cash than better-heeled citizens protected by checkbooks and credit cards. To such holdup men, usually prowling the rundown neighborhoods where they themselves live in back alleys and abandoned houses, any passerby is a possibility.

This type of sudden, drug-crazed theft is less likely to be encountered in even moderately affluent neighborhoods. Such strung-out people cannot afford to live there; traveling there costs at least bus fare; their criminal activity is only erratic and spontaneous as the need for drugs comes upon them. In comfortable neighborhoods, the danger comes much more from clearheaded, calculating criminals who plan their moves and select their sites. If one is going to all this trouble to steal, why select a home put together with hand-me-down furniture and ten-cent-store cutlery? And if the thieves mistakenly enter such a house, why risk backing a pickup to the door just to load it with ten-year-old appliances and furniture only the Good Will Industries would welcome?

Simple life-styles, in fact, offer thieves inordinate risk for piddling gain. Such life-styles proclaim more. They represent concrete evidence that these are not families who indulge themselves lavishly while others go hungry; these are not the favored children of a society which fails to provide for its poor and uneducated. The motivations of criminals are not pricked and excited by the obvious unfairness of life; their hostilities are not fanned by the urge to "get even."

Simple life-styles, particularly among people who obviously have the skills and background to compete successfully in the rat race, proclaim a faith. They advertise a greater value on people-needs than on possessions. At the very least, they show that someone has chosen his occupation by other than material values. To more sensitive observers, they may suggest people who are uncomfortable to use up more than their share of the world's resources, or even people who contribute heavily to humanitarian causes rather than credit accounts.

There is an aura that develops in a home, too. No one will ever know how much of the burglars' decision to leave empty-handed from this one house sprang from practical recognition of the lack of material profit, and how much from some subliminal feeling that this was not the kind of family living they really wanted to disrupt. Some places arouse even in law-abiding visitors a perverse desire to break something, mess things up. Other environments invite calm and tender handling. Some homes charge us with tension, increase our annoyances; others seem to welcome and soothe us even as we step inside the door.

While much of the atmosphere of a house develops from the intangible qualities of the occupants' life-style—the love or hate that permeates relationships, the joy or strain that dominates dispositions, the confidence or fear that marks movements and decisions—the tangible does play its part. Expensive, highly polished, carefully arranged show pieces cry out that here is an environment meant to be seen, not touched; a setting where appearance is more important than human needs.

In role-playing, people often learn that their values are not really what they had thought they were. When neighbors gather together to help one another deal with their fears, they exchange convictions first. Almost everyone says that, faced with an attacker, his or her greatest concern is to avoid personal injury. In the conscious mind, citizens put people before possessions, and they think they mean it.

Yet in role-playing their fears, acting out their dreads and responses, many find they really value possessions above all. There are the women who fight so hard to hold onto their purses that they would surely be slugged. There are the men who risk gunshot just to protect their wallets. There are even stranger aberrancies, such as the adults who, hearing intruders in the house, raced to check on the safety of the new refrigerator, forgetting two small children alone in a bedroom.

An inordinate valuation of things, of possessions, of tangibles, is an invitation to victimization. Priority on people develops an atmosphere of safety. This refrain also runs through the stories of people who came out of dangerous situations unharmed. Jane Addams knew she had no money, despite the opulence of Hull House. No corner of her mind was obsessed with concern for secreted valuables or currency. The ecology worker in New York City could say quite naturally and convincingly, "I work for peace and I don't have any money." Even the two young women in Philadelphia could only come up with ten dollars when pressed, and they had no valuable appurtenances in the apartment which they dared not reveal.

Attackers, thieves, enemies are people too. They respond to what we are; they read much of what we are in the evidences of what we value.

Among the many breathtaking stories of unarmed Quakers on the early frontier, none has received more publicity than that of the unsecured latch-

SAFE PASSAGE ON CITY STREETS

string. Knowing that Indians had been incited by British soldiers to burn and massacre, warned that a war party was coming to destroy their own settlement, Mary and James Tyler could not bring themselves to change the custom by which they consciously proclaimed their faith in love and peace. Hesitating because of their small children, they finally determined to stick with their deeply held faith. They left out the latchstring by which the door could be secured, left it ready for any hand to lift.

In the dark hours of the night, they were wakened by a shattering war whoop. They heard moccasined feet beneath the window; they heard the latch click and the door swing open. By the dying light from their fireplace, they could see seven Indians in full warpaint, could see them motion, confer, and then silently return into the night. In the morning, they looked out upon the smoking ruins of other cabins scattered through the forest.

Perhaps this is the best-known incident because the explanation is in no doubt. Long after the war, James Tyler was sent as a government representative to a conference with the Indians. He told this experience there, and an Indian delegate rose immediately to say, "I was one of that party. We crept up in the night. We meant to burn and kill all. We found the latchstring out. We said, 'We no burn. No kill these people. They do us no harm. They trust Great Spirit.'"

"They do us no harm." Even in today's secularized world, where few victims or attackers have the same overwhelming consciousness of a Divine Spirit, a

70

person's home and possessions and life-style proclaim a great deal about the harm he is capable of
doing, about his depth of concern for human values
compared to material values, about the convictions
in which he really trusts.

Common Sense

Though "atmospheres" about houses and cars do play a part in attracting or repelling invaders, this is a highly intuitive concept and one on which no one can really rely. The reliance on hardware of defense, however, can be carried to such extremes that an atmosphere of fear pervades the owners and a definite challenge is thrown at criminals.

Wall Street analysts estimate that from five thousand to ten thousand companies are now a growth industry in the manufacture and sale of burglar-proofing equipment. Some four hundred million dollars in revenues is predicted for home-security manufacturing and installation firms by 1980. This will represent one dollar paid for security for every four dollars of property stolen. Industrial security is already a four-billion-dollar enterprise. What does all this extravagance actually buy?

Numerous suburban homes are now booby-trapped with electronic devices which go off when the dog scratches, alert the police when a child opens his window, and screech when the husband unlocks the door—all because it is impossible always to remember to de-activate the system. Police tie-ins, at about fifty dollars a month, are disconnected at headquarters because 94 percent of the alarms are false alarms. Batteries burn out and light bulbs fail. Sophisticated burglars cut the main wires and laugh at the naiveté of householders whose elaborate systems merely advertise that they have valuables to protect.

Life in such an electronic fortress is as constricting as that of the poorer person who imprisons himself behind locked doors. To live by choice in a constant awareness of danger and with constant suspicion of every stranger is to subject oneself to exactly the same psychic breakdown that concentration camps deliberately induce.

The stance of confidence and the refusal to move out of one's own world of values and responses do not, however, require one to live in a never-never land as if all the elves were good. To walk down the street counting a roll of bills, or to place an expensive stereo on a table in front of an open first-floor window, is not confidence but stupidity. We may long for the old small-town days when one could start the car on a cold morning and leave it running while going inside to shave. The moral climate of the country *has* changed, and sensible people do not put temptation in the way of every passing adventurer or malcontent.

Similarly, a prudent householder buys good locks

and installs them with long screws. He realizes that secreted keys outside the door will always be found, that lost or stolen keys require an immediate change of locks. He does not carry identification on his key chain, and women do not carry their keys in their purses.

While complicated electronic devices can turn houses into minefields, simple precautions can reduce invitations to burglary without developing paranoia. A timing device to turn on a lamp at dusk is inexpensive, as is the burning of a bathroom light while on vacation. Police say that noise is a great deterrent to intruders, and a low-playing radio uses very little electricity. Even a master switch to light the entire house can be installed beside the bed at relatively little cost.

These are not violence-inducing precautions. They do not threaten, but deter, and they throw no dare to the criminal mind. Similarly, a reasonable prudence in discussing one's plans, possessions, or protections with strangers is only good sense. Parents can teach children not to answer questions over the phone, not to respond to "pollsters" and "researchers."

The most creative approach to the burglary problem is neighborliness. Where neighbors know one another, at least casually, they tend to respond to unusual activities on neighborhood premises. When asked to keep an eye on one another's places during vacations, they feel a real sense of responsibility. In times of extraordinary criminal activity in the area, they can pair up for shopping, alternate walking small children to and from school, meet together to plan group responses or campaign for better lighting. They become known to one another's dogs, and recognize the animals' restlessness and barking when strangers are about.

These precautions are as normal and reasonable as locking the car when parked or cutting off newspaper delivery while on a trip. They are predicated on reducing temptation, on prevention rather than confrontation. They actually increase one's freedom to go in and out on the normal errands of life, and to do so with a sense of community and an increased awareness of the goodness of people as well as their weaknesses. In this spirit, the possibility of reacting calmly and creatively to the completely unpredictable attack is increased.

Stolen Harmonies

On one of the "dangerous" streets of Baltimore, a weird, wacky, wonderful fairy tale took form recently. A woman, sighing for the piano she had never had, touched the heart of her son—one of those angry young men we so often fear. He rushed out of the flat, broke into a building, stole a piano, and began to push it down the street, a gift for the mother who had never had very much.

A piano cannot be camouflaged or hidden in a jacket pocket. Someone saw, reported, and the police soon drove up. The young thief was carried off to jail, but no one had time to send for the piano. In majestic incongruity, it sat alone on the city street.

Baltimore streets are almost empty at night, only an occasional person flitting home from work, a couple dashing from car to doorstep. Eventually one of these rare pedestrians came down the deserted street, saw the piano, stopped, and fingered a chord.

Somehow the chord held him. The chord expanded into a melody; one melody expanded into another.

People began to come out from behind their locked doors, to rub shoulders around the old piano, to join voices in well-known songs. Eleven o'clock, midnight, one o'clock, and the impromptu party went on. Young and old, black and white, people who normally rushed by each other with suspicion or coldness, formed a happy circle of friendliness and sharing and song.

There were no holdups on the street that night. No drug pushing, no burglary, no rape, no murder. Instead, there was a party, a night that residents described as one of the happiest of their lives.

The modern tragedy is that all this simple, human joy had to spring from a theft. A theft, what is more, that probably would not have occurred had the neighborhood been less barren of music and song, sharing and fun—the pleasures of human fellowship.

There are lessons on the streets as surely as there are sermons in stone. Were we to pour forth from our homes, to walk our streets, to visit with neighbors over curbstones and steps and grocery packages, there would be no hiding places for muggers and pushers and rapists and con men. There would be friendly faces and responsive personalities when we were frightened; friendly faces and responsive personalities for growing children to relate to; friendly faces and responsive personalities to laugh away loneliness and suspicion.

We may dream of a simpler life; we may remember

the neighborly streets of small towns where members of my generation grew up safely forty years ago. But we cannot go back. We cannot wipe out the giant cities. We cannot remove the thirst for knowledge which draws people to the massive libraries and museums and theaters only cities provide. We cannot undo the technology that masses thousands of workers in close-packed houses and apartments.

But no technological imperative requires that we become, ourselves, interchangeable cogs, programmed things, isolated products of the city. Every street can become a neighborhood or a hive according to the voluntary actions of the people who reside along it.

Fantasize with me a moment. What would happen to the most dangerous street in your city if human beings sang hymns or ballads or labor songs or even so-called drinking songs under the streetlights? Together. A piano is just a bit too way-out, but the guitars and recorders of the younger generation could accompany tunes all ages know. The harmonicas and even the Jews' harps could come out of old folks' pockets, the mandolins from closets where they now gather dust.

There will be safety on the streets when there are people on the streets. Busy people, happy people, socializing people. People who are not fearful. Anyone who has roamed Union Square in San Francisco at night, or Fisherman's Wharf, or Chinatown, knows that city streets can be festivals, that strangers can greet each other, that laughter can ring in the air. And security increase.

The outer world is but a reflection of our inner world; a reflection which then adds confirmation to that inner world. And so the circle runs its course, result strengthening cause which magnifies result which intensifies cause which multiplies result.

CLASP Your Neighbor

There are not enough peripatetic pianos to re-create neighborliness on American streets. And we are not likely to change our individual habits spontaneously. But a people undeterred by the dangers of a moon voyage can program safe passage across city streets.

Some years ago, the mothers in a few cities got together to make havens for school children. On every block, volunteers who were home during the day agreed to put insignia in their windows. Any child frightened, hurt, or ill could ring those doorbells and be sure of a comforting response. These women kept eyes on the street during the times children passed, and they noted everything from a lurking stranger to a loose dog.

Though this plan had some of the defects of that heart fund drive which once flooded physicians' offices with hysterically induced cardiac cases, it did offer children some sense of community as they walked through strange neighborhoods. As fewer children walk to school, the program is declining, but it served as a model for other cooperative endeavors. Women Organized Against Rape now have their home sanctuary identification sticker as the base of an extensive program to combat rape, the fear of rape, and the traumatizing effects of rape.

Students on a Colorado campus recently plagued by assaults and rapes have adapted the principle. Working in pairs, they offer an escort service to anyone who must cross campus alone at night. Though this service, too, represents a constant reminder of danger, it does reduce the incidence of attacks, increase night use of libraries and other facilities, and bring together many students who might otherwise be only nameless faces to each other.

More positively oriented efforts have been made by small groups of concerned citizens acting without fanfare or identification. A few years ago, a service-minded group in New York City put people on the streets in pairs late at night. Walking in really deprived areas, they picked up winos before they could be abused, took them home, and dried them out. They escorted lonely walkers, and gave beds to runaways. And they were a visible presence where young toughs loitered in doorways.

There is a ghetto street in Washington, D.C. unobtrusively patrolled and watched by older male residents. These men have no authority, and they wear no insignia. But they are there—eyes upon the street and upon every passerby. The attack rate in that neighborhood approaches zero, although two streets away the crime rate is among the highest in the capital.

Protection is only half the solution. Working as groups, some people have gone beyond protection to positive community-building. A few city churches have turned on the lights, opened up doors, enlisted members to be present as song leaders, coffee makers, library helpers, and listening ears.

Where this has happened, neighborhoods open up. People coming to and from these centers of activity must pass along the sidewalks. Their very numbers on the street reduce the incidence of attack. Apartment dwellers who meet in the rec room call to each other later on the streets, walk along together when they meet. Young people coming to sing meet older people coming to read; lonely newcomers to the area meet residents who have gathered because nowhere else can they visit together without a cover charge.

Neighborhood schools are sometimes used this way, Y's, or the conference rooms behind branch libraries. Any facility that can offer a quiet reading room for students and older people, a casual rapping room, a game room, a music room, or a listening corner can become a center for people of all ages. With separate rooms for diverse interests, a whole cross-section of the population also blends together in the common foyers and around the common coffeepot. The presence of a few dedicated people to handle practical oversight and to talk with the lonely or listen to the lost makes a kind of neighborhood home. Not a professional clinic, but a family atmosphere is the healing needed by normal people.

The Citizens Local Alliance for a Safer Philadelphia (CLASP) unites over sixty small groups and organizations trying to eliminate the causes of fear and, inevitably linked, the causes of crime. They have recognized what most of us overlook. The absence of citizens on the streets has increased the danger surrounding police officers themselves, and thus contributed both to police negligence and to police brutality. Police, too, are human beings walking the streets in fear. The disappearance of citizens from those streets decreases their professionalism and increases their human weaknesses.

Fanning out to work at the neighborhood level, CLASP organizes blocks. At block meetings, residents come to know one another and to develop a sense of kinship. They recognize one another on the streets, and are more likely to feel personal concern for one another. This in turn gives a sense of security to each even when alone—behind the next door is an acquaintance, a potential ally.

How much of our escalating personal fear springs from just this lack in today's living? Getting off a night bus, starting down the street, we see a shadowy figure approaching. Added to our fear that this figure may be a mugger is the terror that no window observer will interfere, no human being will answer our scream, no door will open to our knock. Indeed, we would be as frightened to run up the nearest steps as to approach the pedestrian; we would not dare to enter a stranger's flat and so put ourselves at his mercy. He, behind his closed door, might rob, rape, or beat us.

In making block residents known to each other, CLASP has put an end to this horrible sense of isolation and suspicion of our fellows. It has made the streets into associations of acquaintances. These associations have turned minds into creative channels as residents "brainstorm" together about their common problems. Women have begun to shop together, to pick up children together, to carry the irreplaceable house keys and driver's license on their persons so that purses may be relinquished more easily. Many houses now have a chain of bells hanging from the ceiling, to be set swinging by any opening of the door. Porch lights are turned on at dusk, some by electronic devices, to increase street illumination and to advertise that this is a neighborhood that cares.

CLASP has moved beyond mere introductions to positive programs for reformation. A block association deliberately puts "walkers" on the streets at all hours of the day and night. In pairs, these walkers move around the block, speaking to everyone, observing loiterers and dark corners. They are armed only with notebooks listing the names and addresses of people who will let them use their phones. In some blocks, elderly people who cannot participate in the walking keep coffee and snacks waiting, and these older citizens look forward to the friendly visiting of walkers dropping in to warm up, to telephone, to chat.

Young people have been helped to set up centers. Taking the responsibility for these havens offers them experience in meaningful planning and problem-solving, helps build a sense of community among the young. Youth centers offer an inexpensive evening of human warmth, and so reduce the number of bored young people aimlessly wandering in search of diversion. Racial tensions have also been reduced as black and white youth come together in the friendly, nonrestrictive atmosphere.

To deal directly with the crime problem, the Block Associations have developed simple alert systems by which threatened residents can quickly rally their neighbors. (Descriptive brochures are available from Citizens' Alliance for a Safer Philadelphia, 1500 Chestnut St., Room 402, Philadelphia 19102.) A simple hand-operated horn is supplied to all. On the streets, people carry them inconspicuously. At home, people keep them ready at the door. When one nervous pedestrian sounds her horn, householders step to their porches and add the sound of their own sirens. To the warning of an endangered person's siren is added a chorus which proclaims *she is not alone!*

This plan does not escalate violence. It does frighten off attackers, alert help, and build a reputation that the neighborhood is a cooperating unit. The criminal element tends to avoid such neighborhoods in favor of more vulnerable areas.

The police, of course, know of these signals. More creatively, the Blocks are trying to knit the police themselves into fellowship. Some Blocks are planning a little ceremony in which to present a horn to one police officer symbolically in order to dramatize the residents' desire to come to the aid of police persons too.

Some associations have organized workshops in which residents receive instruction in safety procedures for home, school, and street. Coming together to solve the common, immediate problem of street crime, residents build positive bonds of mutual support.

Furthermore, a broader civic participation generally develops. Block groups, drawn together first by common fear, have pressured city governments for improved street lighting and addict services. In preparing these campaigns, they have learned the techniques of effective community action and thus begun to take back into their own hands some of the decision making by which cities live.

A community of people who feel some power over the conditions of their own lives is a community likely to exert power right at the doorstep level. Children are better supervised; troublesome adults are reasoned with; each individual polices himself more rigorously.

In West Philadelphia CLASP neighborhoods, signs of such improvement have become countable. Homeownership is increasing; crime is significantly decreasing. The community develops programs to aid small businessmen, to reduce unemployment, to shut out drugs, to enrich the lives of the elderly. Some block organizations are now helping families in crisis and mentally disturbed residents.

All of these activities are intrinsically helpful. The greatest deterrent to victimization, however, is the more subtle but pervasive change in the attitudes of all the people along a block. They begin to lose the corrosive fear which has constricted their personalities and blighted their reactions to other human beings. They are warmed by the friendliness around them, reminded of the good that is in other people. They come to look for—and often find—the basic warmth in anyone else they meet.

This attitude of freedom to be oneself, and of respect for other selves, is as we have seen, the greatest protective device a person can have.

Mental Nutrition

Ross Flanagan of CLASP says about personal safety, "There isn't any alternative to changing your life-style."

Block organizations work on the principle that people change or grow when they are personally involved with others in mutual problem solving. Therefore, neighborhoods are helped to connect people, enable them to rediscover that old sense of community, offer them a group in which to share ideas and try out new ways of coping with common problems.

Certainly change is easier in association with other warm human beings. It is not impossible alone, however, as prophets and saints and leaders down through the ages have proven. One is not at the mercy of every hoodlum in the city just because his neighborhood is not a gathered community. Neither is the person from a gathered community helpless when he or she leaves that neighborhood, or travels to another city.

Ultimately, each of us does walk our lonesome valley, and what we have to give to the neighborhoods and communities around us depends upon the strength we have in the privacy of our own souls, the life-style that we have adopted in the individuality of our own convictions.

In a large city, a woman who had devoted her life to the peaceful resolution of conflict at all levels of living found herself overtaken by two young men. They came up from behind and separated significantly at her shoulders. Her arms were loaded with shopping bags, and she was far from any residence where she was known.

Before they could enclose her, before they could speak a word, she beamed from one to the other, thrust out her packages, and told them how glad she was that they had come along.

"I was rather nervous on this street—and these bags are so heavy. Would you help me?"

Instinctively, they took the packages. The three then walked along together while the woman cheerily thanked them and told them how good they were to help.

Her life-style had been formed over many years, and she reached out automatically to the normal decency and helpfulness dormant in everyone. She was able to tap that helpfulness without need of an organized block at her back or a siren in her fingers.

Another person who had long before changed his life-style to value people over property met an armed holdup man as he emerged from a bus station. Ignoring the gun and the mutter, he burst out with concern.

"It's cold. Why don't you take my jacket?"

And as the gunman fumbled, he continued naturally, "I was just going for something to eat. Why don't you join me?" He even offered the holdup man some money, but at this stage in their relationship, it was refused.

These were people whose lives had been devoted to peaceful human relations, to the search for creative means of resolving conflict, to work for reconciliation among individuals, groups, races and nations. Their spontaneous actions under pressure sprang from that on which they had fed.

We are what we eat—mentally, emotionally, and spiritually as well as physically. People who feed their inner selves on the literature of violence, the conversation of fear, the planning of retaliation, and the fantasies of quick draw and sudden uppercuts, escalate violence in any encounter. These are the desperate merchants who grab a gun from under the cash register and frighten the thief into shooting. These are the women who swing their handbags at the mugger's ear and are beaten in return.

The violent enter the criminal's scenario as fully as the terrified. For each, the criminal is programmed. When threat meets threat, we can count upon it that the criminal's level of retaliation will be more brutal than that of an ordinary citizen. The criminal has already accepted the ethic of violence and death; to act it out is almost a release.

Something of the sort also happens to otherwise respectable citizens who feed themselves on violence in fiction and in fact. Their imaginations become busy with defenses and sharpshooting and sudden blows. They visualize scenes in which they knock out an attacker just like a TV detective, or put a bullet through an escaping holdup man like a movie Westerner. They read crime reports and imagine how they would have thwarted the mugger —and left him sorry he ever met them. They begin to experience a kind of lust for punishing criminals.

This is a principle as easy to test as the results of physical nutrition. Stuff yourself with cakes, pies, sweet drinks, and little else for a few days, and you will notice a difference in your body, in your sense of well being, in your mental alertness, in your disposition. Stuff yourself with detective stories and crime reports and TV shoot-em-ups for a few days, reading and watching little else, and you will find a coarsening in your attitudes, a suspicion in your responses. You will walk the streets alert for trouble; you will plan sudden blows and quick jabs as loiterers catch your attention. You may begin to carry guns or weights or knives in your clothing.

We are what we feed upon, but fortunately, we can choose what we feed upon. There is absolutely no guarantee that any regimen or any attitude will give 100 percent protection against criminal attack. But there is an almost 100 percent certainty that particular attitudes will increase the chances of being attacked, and increase the chances of being injured during attack.

The stories of those who showed no fear in the presence of an attacker are marked also by their showing no resistance. There are two programs to which the criminal is plugged in: fear and violence. He knows how to play on the nerves of the terrified, reaping massive ego satisfaction from their terror. He is excited by terror. He knows also how to counter the violent, to out-slug, out-beat, out-cut, and out-shoot amateur John Waynes. He is challenged by counter-attack. Citizens who have programmed themselves for self-defensive violence carry about them an aura which invites violence. They are a provocation to criminals; they invite put-down from those who have made toughness a way of life.

Certainly not all men who do regular push-ups and jog for fitness are developing aggressive attitudes. A feeling of physical fitness improves one's mental and emotional poise, may increase one's basic self-confidence in all situations. Not all young women now enrolling in karate or judo schools are fantasizing bone-breaking blows or spine-dislocating throws. For some young women, the discovery that they have physical power and body control is the first step toward really respecting themselves as autonomous human beings. As autonomous, self-determined human beings, both men and women are freed to make creative, violence-reducing responses to dangerous situations.

Faith in one's physical prowess as a club against others, however, is a different matter. In a very real sense, every person does live by faith, and every faith becomes self-justifying. Faith in violence calls

92

forth violence, in oneself and in others. This type of response occurs at all levels of encounter.

The virile, young male teacher who enters his first classroom in the faith that he can out-muscle any obstreperous adolescent, will find himself faced with obstreperous adolescents. His very swagger, his blatant belief that they need "a strong hand," and that he is just the guy to apply it, challenges the unruly to show him that he is mistaken. Adolescents have their own self-image to maintain, their own faith in toughness.

In my own city, where the police confiscate hundreds of guns and knives from the high schools each year, the papers rarely have a story of physical violence against a woman teacher. Not all male teachers, of course, live by faith in their ability to dominate physically. Not all male teachers escalate student violence. But no woman teacher does. Women teachers must have faith in peaceful and psychological forms of control or they dare not enter a city classroom at all. The teachers who are physically abused are men, except in rare cases of rape. A little questioning usually reveals that they are proudly athletic men with great faith in their own physical strength as the ultimate weapon of control. And TV-trained juveniles respond in kind. How much more does the stickup man or the mugger respond in kind? His faith in the power of fist and weapon is absolute.

We build our faith by the information with which we saturate our consciousnesses. And we all "act out" that upon which our minds are feeding. The 70 percent of all homicides which occur between family members and friends also represent the dominance of our mental nutrition over our casually proclaimed principles, the self-fulfilling nature of our real faith. The man who has prepared himself for burglars with a gun under his pillow is the one who grabs that gun in the heat of a family argument. The woman who has preplanned the number of steps to her carving knife in case of an intruder is the one who uses that knife when a neighbor threatens to report her child to the police. The youth who has practiced a sudden savage blow to the neck of an assailant is the one who fells a friend accusing him of card cheating. If our mental and emotional nutrition determines our responses in these close relationships, how much more does this nutrition signal the criminal that here is one who must be killed before he kills?

Yet we control this nutritional aura, even if we live among the most unneighborly. Just as we can choose food which imparts to us a noticeable glow of health and vitality, so we can choose mental and emotional diets which impart an unmistakable aura of peace and goodwill. Our attitudes will become conciliatory but not helpless, our responses creative rather than destructive, our aura one of confident goodwill rather than defensive violence.

A woman who unwisely allowed a canvassing roofer into her home soon recognized that he was emotionally disturbed and that his uncalled for prowling through her house was a search for evidence of her solitariness. Yet she had fed herself on literature of Jane Addamses and Gandhis, and she was truly moved by the story of woe he poured out as he pushed into rooms and closets. So she sympathized genuinely with his problems, and she prayed for him as he moved jerkily from her to some other door and back. Though his recital of problems became more and more sexual, she remained calm. She did not go near the phone lest he panic. She kept her arms casually crossed and relaxed. And she readily agreed to have him do the minor outside repair job which had led to his admittance.

After half an hour of listening to his disturbing stories, she worked him again to the door, and at last, out. She was ready with a check on the doorstep when his two shabby helpers clambered down off her roof.

An hour later, she went out to mail a letter. As she reached the sidewalk, she saw them. They sat in a plain car, not a name-printed truck, a few yards from her house. They pointed toward her, obviously discussing her. So she nodded, waved slightly, and hurried on to the mailbox a few blocks away. When she returned, they were still there; again she nodded quickly and hurried inside. Not until the car left did she emerge to justify her suspicion that no real work had been done on the roof.

Whatever their plan, she had lost nothing but some rather uncomfortable minutes and an equal number of dollars. She was safe. And over the ensuing weeks, as the memory faded, she was not revisited nor broken in upon.

We cannot know how the encounter would have

played itself out had she become defensive, had she challenged the man's very personal revelations, had she reached toward the phone or raced for the door. Emotionally disturbed men react violently to small provocation or implied slight. Even had he come with no malevolent purpose, his self-esteem might well have demanded that he manifest control of the situation.

Instead, she treated him with respect and responded with quiet sympathy to his very real unhappiness. She maintained distance, but the distance of the understanding outsider. She enabled him to leave her house with the facade of business encounter preserved, with his emotions calmed rather than exacerbated.

No alarm system, no gun under the pillow, or knife in the drawer can protect one in these lonely encounters. By the time one is positive she is dealing with a criminal, it is too late to reach these weapons. To use them before one is positive is to risk humiliation at the least, the commission of attack or murder upon an innocent at the worst.

The inner weapons of confidence, goodwill, a firmly rooted self—these no law can confiscate and no intruder appropriate. They cannot be turned against oneself, nor are they ever out of reach. They are, in short, "what we are," and they determine in large measure what we attract from the world of people and experiences about us.

DATE DUE

12-13-77	APR 2 8 1998		
MAR 3 1 1979			
APR 1 4 1979			
JUN 2 0 1979			
APR 8 1980			
APR 4 1981			
6-16-8			
MAR 3 0 1982			
JUN 4 1982			
JUL 2 0 1982			
AUG - 2 1982			
FEB 1 9 1984			
4/28/88			
3/25/91			
JUN 2 4 1994			
MAR 2 1 1996			
APR 1 7 1996			
NOV 1 2 1997			
GAYLORD			PRINTED IN U.S.A